From Cells to Systems

Rebecca L. Johnson

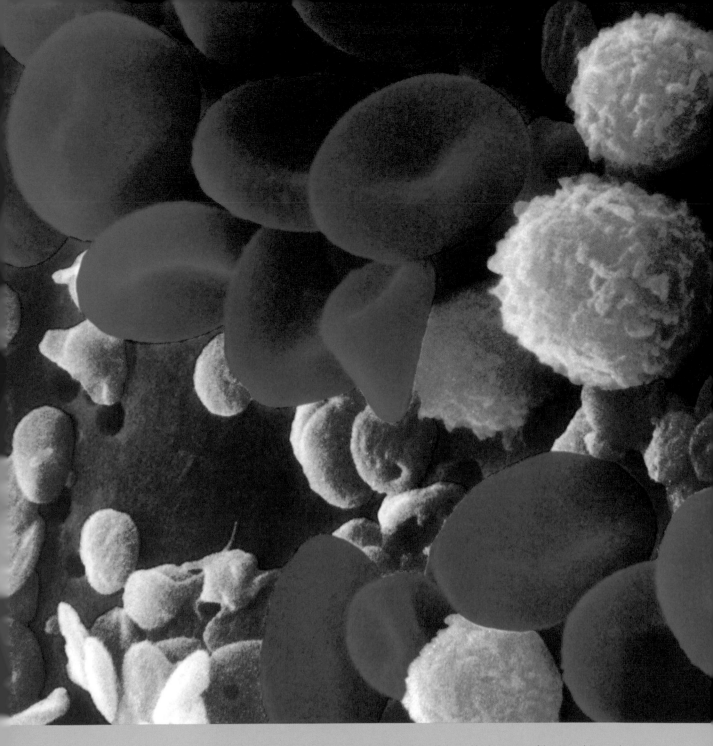

PICTURE CREDITS

Cover (front), 32 Biophoto Associates/Photo Researchers, Inc.; 2-3 NIH/Science Source/Photo Researchers, Inc.; 4-5 (top), 6-7 (middle), 10 (bottom) Eric V. Grave/Photo Researchers, Inc.; 4-5 (bottom), 6-7 (background), 26 (bottom) Taxi/Getty Images; 5 (top), 34 (second from top) Photodisc Green/Getty Images; 5 (bottom) Allsport/Getty Images; 6-7 (top) Hank Morgan/Photo Researchers, Inc.; 6-7 (bottom) Innerspace Imaging/Photo Researchers, Inc.; 7 (background), 8-9 (background), 12-13 (background), 14-15 (background) David McCarthy/Photo Researchers, Inc.; 9 (left), 34 (middle) CNRI/Photo Researchers, Inc.; 9 (middle) Science Photo Library/Photo Researchers, Inc.; 9 (right), 19 (left), 30 (bottom left) Susumu Nishinaga/Photo Researchers, Inc.; 10 (top), 19 (right) Lester V. Bergman/Corbis; 12 (bottom), 22 (bottom) Stockdisc Classic/Getty Images; 15 Allsport Concepts/Getty Images; 16-17 David Edwards/National Geographic Image Collection; 19 (middle) Nibsc/Photo Researchers, Inc.; 20 Michael Keller/Corbis; 25 (top left), 30 (top left) SPL/Photo Researchers, Inc.; 25 (top right), 35 (bottom) Dachez/Photo Researchers, Inc.; 26 (top) The Image Bank/Getty Images; 28 (top) Massimo Listri/Corbis; 28 (bottom) Omikron/Photo Researchers, Inc.; 29 (top) John Heseltine/Photo Researchers, Inc.; 29 (bottom) Brian Yarvin/Photo Researchers, Inc.; 30 (top right) Image 100/Getty Images; 30 (bottom right) Rubberball Productions/Getty Images; 31 (top left), 34 (bottom) Michelle D. Bridwell/PhotoEdit; 31 (middle left) Stem Jems/Photos Researchers, Inc.; 31 (middle right) Royalty-Free Corbis; 31 (bottom left) Photodisc Blue/Getty Images; 31 (bottom right) Digital Vision/Getty Images; 35 (second from top) Keith R. Porter/Photo Researchers, Inc.; 36 (bottom right) SPL/Photo Researchers, Inc.

Produced through the worldwide resources of the National Geographic Society, John M. Fahey, Jr., President and Chief Executive Officer; Gilbert M. Grosvenor, Chairman of the Board; Nina D. Hoffman, Executive Vice President and President, Books and Education Publishing Group.

PREPARED BY NATIONAL GEOGRAPHIC SCHOOL PUBLISHING

Ericka Markman, Senior Vice President and President, Children's Books and Education Publishing Group; Steve Mico, Senior Vice President, Editorial Director, Publisher; Francis Downey, Executive Editor; Richard Easby, Editorial Manager; Bea Jackson, Director of Layout and Design; Jim Hiscott, Design Manager; Cynthia Olson, Art Director; Margaret Sidlosky, Illustrations Director; Matt Wascavage, Manager of Publishing Services; Sean Philpotts, Jane Ponton, Production Managers; Ted Tucker, Production Specialist.

MANUFACTURING AND QUALITY CONTROL

Christopher A. Liedel, Chief Financial Officer; Phillip L. Schlosser, Director; Clifton M. Brown III, Manager

CONSULTANT AND REVIEWER

W. Michael Panneton, Professor of Pharmacological and Physiological Science, Saint Louis University School of Medicine

BOOK DEVELOPMENT

Amy Sarver

◄ Different kinds of cells make up the blood in your body.

Contents

BOOK DESIGN/PHOTO RESEARCH
3R1 Group, Inc.

Copyright © 2006 National Geographic Society.
All Rights Reserved. Reproduction of the whole or any part of the
contents without written permission from the publisher is prohibited.
National Geographic, National Geographic School Publishing,
National Geographic Reading Expeditions, and the Yellow Border
are registered trademarks of the National Geographic Society.

Published by the National Geographic Society
1145 17th Street N.W.
Washington, D.C. 20036-4688

ISBN-13: 978-0-7922-5410-2
ISBN-10: 0-7922-5410-4

2012
      6 7 8 9 10 11 12 13 14 15

Printed in Canada.

Looking At Cells

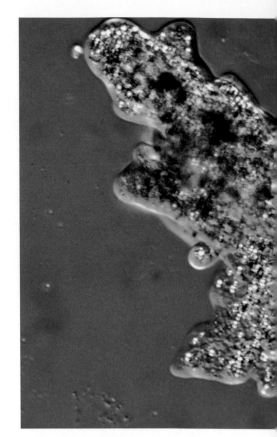

▲ **An amoeba has one cell.**

All living things are made of **cells.** Your body is made of cells. A bird and a tree are also made of cells. Different living things have different numbers of cells. Small animals have fewer cells than large animals.

- An amoeba is just one cell in size.
- A worm can have thousands of cells.
- A bird has millions of cells.
- Your body has trillions of cells.

Look at the photos. How are these living things alike and different?

....
cell – the smallest living part of a plant or animal

▲ **A bird has millions of cells.**

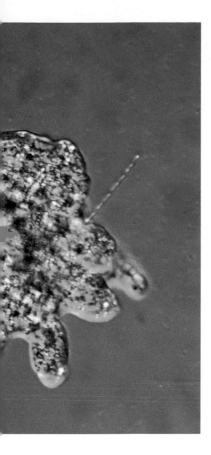

▲ A worm can have thousands of cells.

▲ Your body has trillions of cells.

Big Idea
Your body is made of
cells that work together.

Set Purpose
Learn how cells in your
body work together.

Questions You Will Explore

How do cells work together in
your body?

What jobs do cells do in your body?

▲ Muscle cells
in the arm

◀ Nerve cells
in the brain

▼ Bone cells
in the hand

How Do Cells Work Together?

Cells in your body are very small. But each cell does not work alone. Cells work together.

Just think about doing a chin-up. Nerve cells work together to send messages through your body. Bone cells work together to support, or hold up, your body. Muscle cells work together to move your body. In this book, you will learn about cells and how they work together in your body.

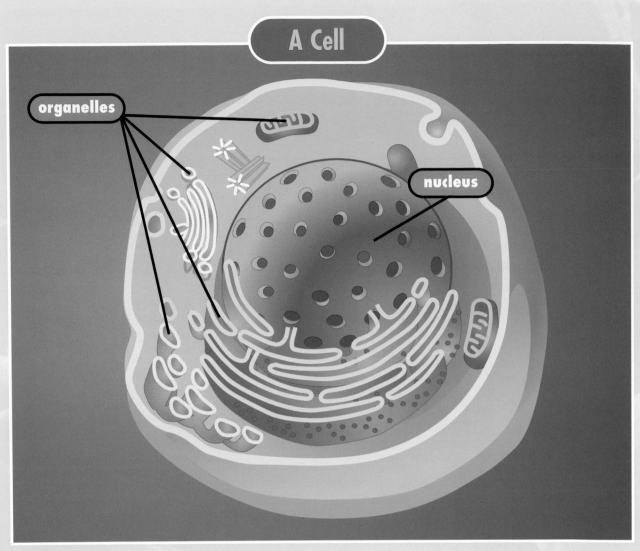

organelles

nucleus

▲ **This diagram shows some parts of a cell.**

How Cells Are Alike

There are many different kinds of cells. Each kind of cell does a different job. Yet all cells are alike in some ways. Cells have a **nucleus**. The nucleus tells the cell what to do. All cells also have **organelles**. Each kind of organelle has a different job to do. Organelles do jobs that help cells live.

nucleus – the part of a cell that tells the cell what to do

organelle – a part of a cell that does a certain job within the cell

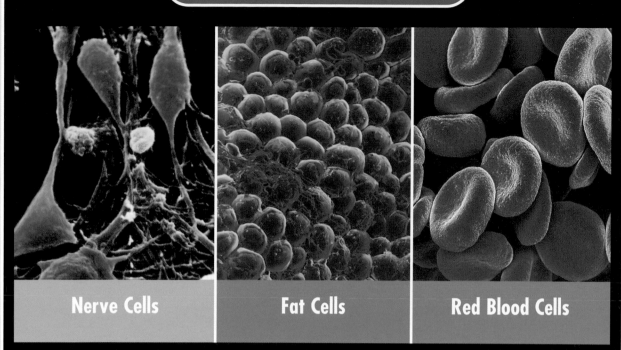

Different Kinds of Cells

Nerve Cells | **Fat Cells** | **Red Blood Cells**

How Cells Are Different

Cells have a nucleus and organelles. But there are many kinds of cells. Each kind of cell is different from other kinds.

Your body has many different kinds of cells. For example, you have nerve cells, fat cells, and blood cells. Different kinds of cells have different jobs to do. The size and shape of a cell depends on its job.

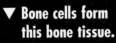
▼ Bone cells form this bone tissue.

Cells Form Tissues

Cells do a lot of work in your body. Yet each cell cannot do much on its own. For example, one bone cell cannot support your body. To support your body, many bone cells must work together.

A group of cells that work together to do a job is called a **tissue**. Bone cells form bone tissue. There are many kinds of tissues in your body.

▲ Bone cells

....

tissue – a group of cells that work together

| Brain | Lungs | Heart |

Tissues Form Organs

Tissues do many jobs. But there are some jobs tissues cannot do on their own. Tissues work together to do bigger jobs. A group of tissues that work together to do a job is an **organ**.

Your body has many organs. Your brain, lungs, and heart are organs. The tissues in your brain work together to control your body. The tissues in your lungs work together to let you breathe. The tissues in your heart work together to move blood through your body. These are just a few of the organs that do jobs in your body.

organ – a group of tissues that does a job in the body

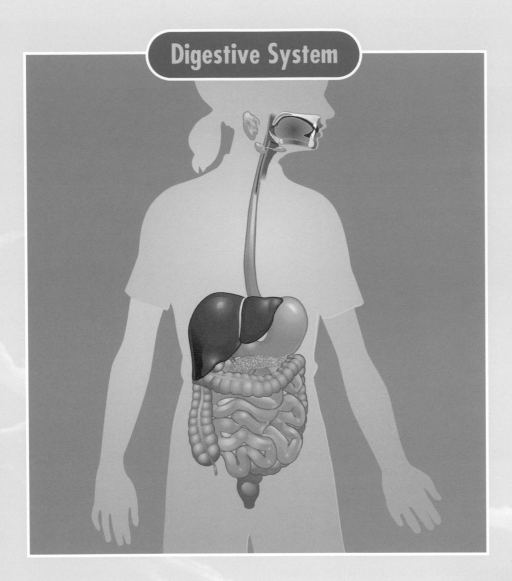

◀ **The digestive system breaks down the food you eat.**

Organs Form Systems

Some jobs are too big for just one organ. A group of organs can work together to form a **system.** A system can do a big job for the body.

The digestive system is a group of organs that work together to break down food. Food gives your body the **nutrients** it needs to live and grow.

system – a group of organs that work together

nutrient – a substance in food that your body needs to live and grow

12

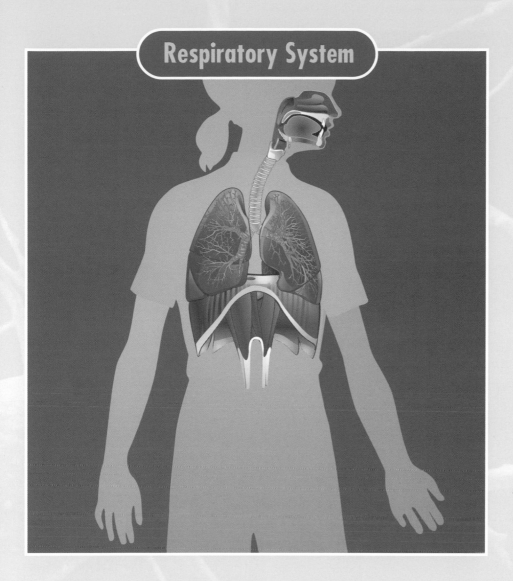

Respiratory System

◀ **The respiratory system moves air into and out of the body.**

A System for Breathing

The respiratory system is a group of organs that move gases into and out of your body.

When you breathe, you take in **oxygen.** Oxygen is a gas that is in the air. The cells in your body need oxygen to live. When you breathe out, you get rid of **carbon dioxide.** Carbon dioxide is a gas that your cells give off as waste.

....

oxygen – a gas needed by cells

carbon dioxide – a gas that is given off by cells

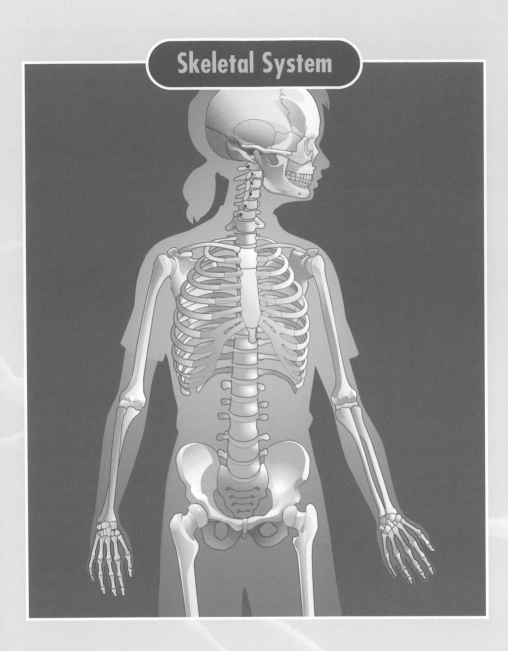

Skeletal System

◀ The skeletal system
supports and
protects your body.

A System for Support

Your body's skeletal system is made of all the
bones in your body. Your bones work together
to support your body. Without bones, you
would not be able to stand up or move.

The skeletal system also protects other parts of
your body. For example, the bones in your chest
protect your heart and lungs. The bones in your
head protect your brain. The bones in your
skeletal system work together to do many jobs.

▲ Your body has systems for moving and doing many other activities.

A Body of Systems

Your body has many systems. Each system does a different job. You have a system for breathing. You have a system for digesting food. You have a system of bones to help you stand up. These are just a few of the systems in your body. The systems in your body work together. Together they keep you alive and healthy.

Stop and Think!

How do cells work together in a system?

Recap
Explain how cells,
tissues, and organs
work together.

Set Purpose
Learn how the parts
of your circulatory
system work together.

A System That Moves

On a bicycle, you can pedal fast. You can feel your heart beat inside your chest. Yet you do not have to ride a bike to make your heart beat. Your heart is always beating. Your heart is part of a system that moves blood through your body.

A Body of Cells

Your body is made of trillions of cells. Each cell is a living thing. All cells need oxygen and other materials to stay alive.

How do the cells in your body get what they need? They get what they need from blood. Blood brings oxygen and other materials to your cells.

▼ Blood carries oxygen and other materials to body cells.

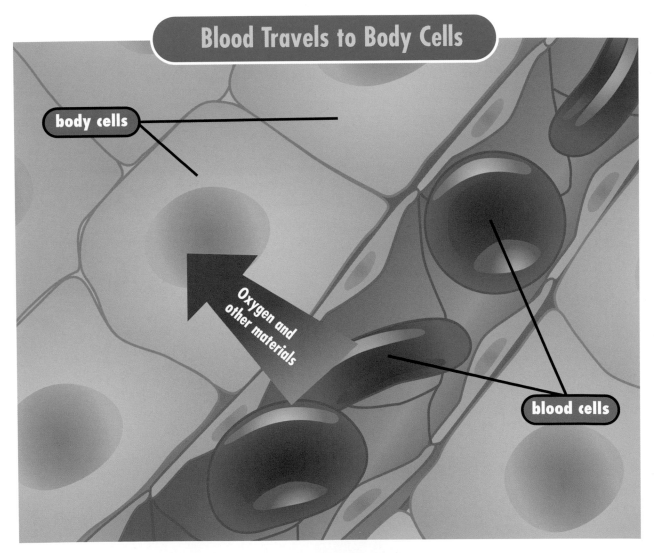

Blood Travels to Body Cells

body cells

Oxygen and other materials

blood cells

Cells in Blood

Blood is a liquid that carries special cells. The liquid part of blood is called plasma. Plasma carries red blood cells, white blood cells, and platelets.

Each type of blood cell does a job for the body. Red blood cells carry oxygen to other cells in the body. White blood cells kill germs that get into your body. Platelets help stop bleeding if you get a cut.

Different Blood Cells

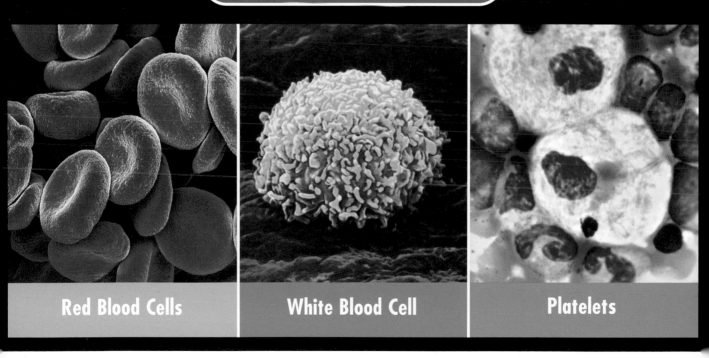

| Red Blood Cells | White Blood Cell | Platelets |

The Heart

The cells in your body depend on blood. Blood provides the things cells need. But what moves the blood around your body? Your heart!

Your heart is an organ that pumps blood. When the heart pumps blood, it makes a sound. This sound is your heartbeat. A doctor listens to your heartbeat to make sure your heart is working as it should.

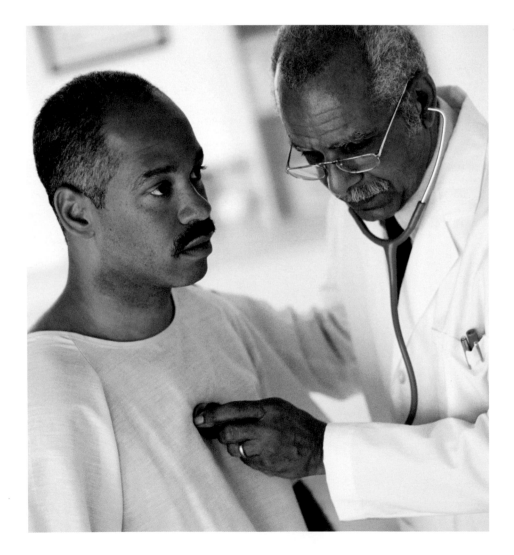

◄ A doctor listens to your heartbeat to make sure your heart is working properly.

Moving Blood

Your heart pumps all day and all night. It never rests. Each day, your heart beats about 100,000 times.

How does the heart work? Blood enters the heart. Then muscles in the heart tighten. This sends the blood out of the heart. The blood then flows through your body.

How the Heart Pumps Blood

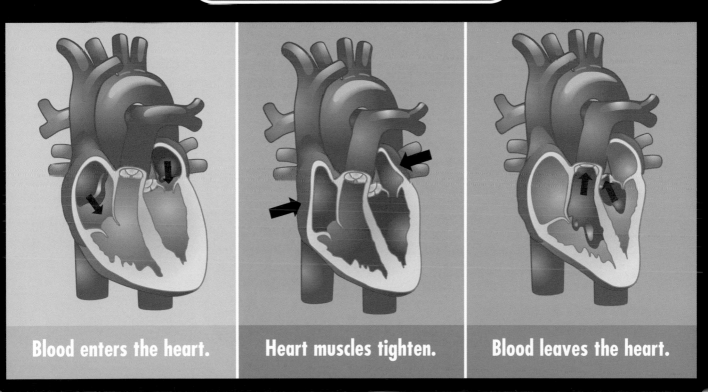

| Blood enters the heart. | Heart muscles tighten. | Blood leaves the heart. |

Blood Vessels

Where does the blood go once it leaves the heart? Blood travels through tubes called **blood vessels.** Some blood vessels take blood to the lungs. That is where blood picks up oxygen. Some blood vessels carry blood to other cells in your body. That is where blood picks up carbon dioxide and delivers oxygen.

....

blood vessel – a tube that carries blood through the body

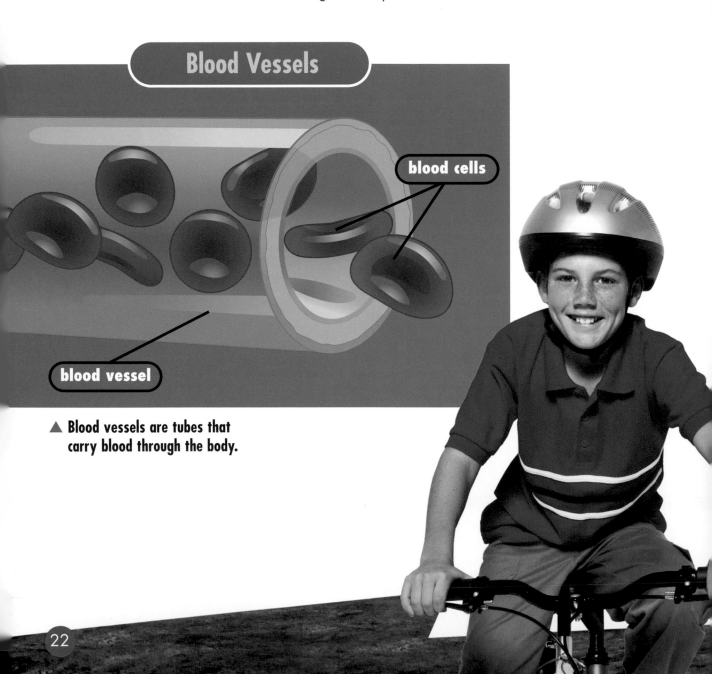

Blood Vessels

blood cells

blood vessel

▲ Blood vessels are tubes that carry blood through the body.

The Circulatory System

Blood vessels and the heart make up the circulatory system. This system is made of organs that move blood through your body. Your heart is the organ that pumps blood. Your blood vessels are the organs that carry blood to every part of your body. Together they keep your blood flowing.

heart

blood vessels

Stop and Think!

HOW do the parts of the circulatory system work together?

Make
Connections

Recap
Explain how the circulatory system moves blood through your body.

Set Purpose
Read these articles to learn more about the cells and systems in your body.

CONNECT WHAT YOU HAVE LEARNED

Cells and Systems

Your body is made of cells that work together. All living things are made up of cells. Here are some ideas you learned about cells, tissues, organs, and systems.

- Your body is made up of cells.
- Cells that work together to do a job are called a tissue.
- Tissues that work together to do a job are called an organ.
- Organs that work together to do a job are called a system.

Check What You Have Learned

HOW do cells, tissues, and organs work together in the body?

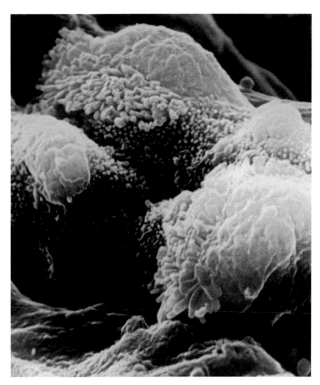

▲ These are lung cells.

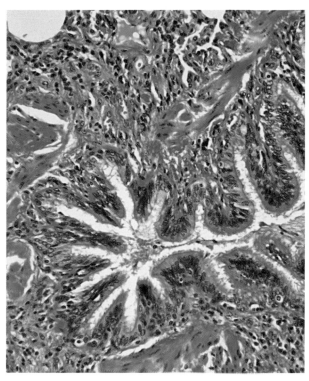

▲ The cells in this lung tissue work together.

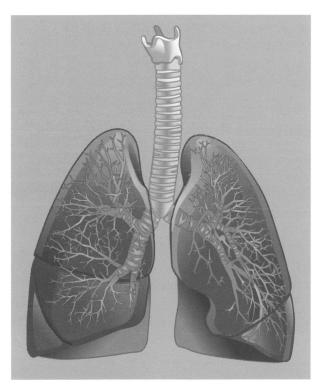

▲ The lungs are organs made of tissues that work together.

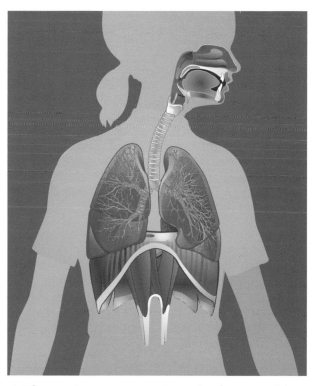

▲ The respiratory system is made of organs that work together.

▲ Your ears are sense organs that let you hear.

Sensing Your World

Can you name your five senses? They are sight, smell, hearing, taste, and touch. Sense organs give you these senses. Your eyes, nose, ears, tongue, and skin are sense organs. Your sense organs give you information about the world around you.

◀ Taste buds on your tongue are sense organs that let you taste food.

Plant Cells

All plants and animals are made of cells. Each plant and animal cell has a nucleus and organelles. Yet a plant cell and animal cell have some differences. A plant cell has organelles called chloroplasts. They let the plant make its own food. A plant cell also has a thick cell wall. This makes the plant cell strong and tough.

▼ **Animal cell**

organelles

nucleus

▼ **Plant cell**

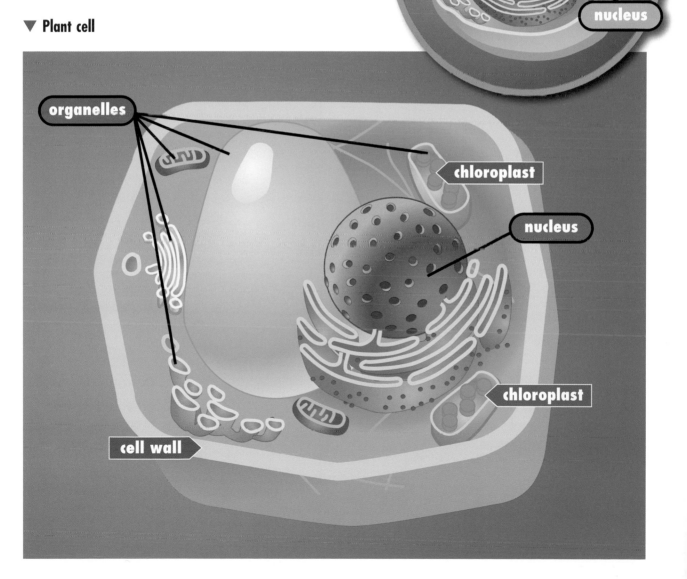

organelles

chloroplast

nucleus

chloroplast

cell wall

27

Learning About Cells

Long ago, people did not know that living things were made of cells. People did not learn about cells until microscopes were invented. Microscopes are tools that let people see very small things.

The first microscopes were made in the 1600s. They were simple. But they let people study living things like never before. In 1665, an English scientist named Robert Hooke looked at a thin piece of cork under his microscope. The cork had tiny parts that reminded Hooke of small rooms called cells. So he named the parts cells. People have used the word cells ever since!

▶ Hooke drew these pictures of the cork cells he saw with his microscope.

▲ Microscopes are tools that let people see very small things.

▲ Oranges are one kind of food that help keep your cells healthy.

Healthy Cells

Your cells get materials they need from the food you eat. So it is important to eat a healthful diet.

Eating good food helps keep the cells in your body healthy. Cells make up every part of your body. That means eating right keeps tissues, organs, and systems healthy, too.

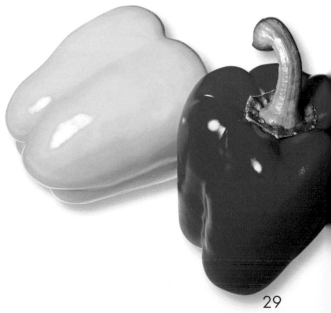

Many kinds of words are used in this book. Here you will learn about homophones. You will also learn about root words and derivatives.

Homophones

Homophones are words that sound the same but have different meanings. Find the homophones below. Then write a new sentence for each homophone.

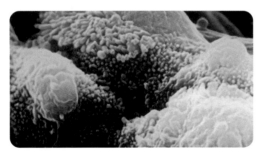

Cells work together in a tissue.

She **sells** flowers.

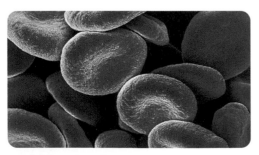

Red blood cells carry carbon dioxide given off as **waste.**

He wears the belt around his **waist.**

Root Words and Derivatives

Some words are root words. They can be used to make other words. A new word made from a root word is called a derivative. Find the root words and derivatives below.

His body **digests** food.

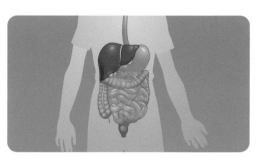

The **digestive** system breaks down food.

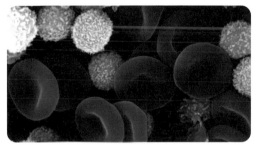

Cells can be **different** shapes.

There are **differences** between plants and animals.

She takes a deep **breath.**

His **breathing** is fast when he runs.

Research and Write

Write About a Cell

Choose one kind of cell in your body. Research where the cells are found in the body. Then write a paragraph telling what you learned.

Research

Collect books and reference materials, or go online.

Read and Take Notes

As you read, take notes and draw pictures.

Write

Imagine that you are the cell you researched. Write a paragraph telling where you are located and what you do. Include sentences about other cells you work with in a tissue, an organ, and a system.

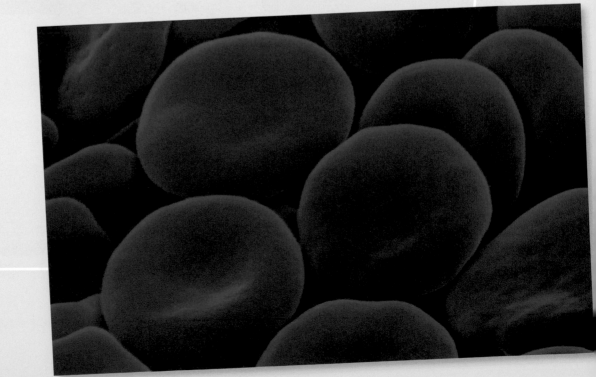

Read and Compare

Read More About Cells and Systems

Find and read other books about cells and systems in the body. As you read, think about these questions.

- How are cells important in the human body?
- How do cells work together in the body?
- How do scientists learn about cells and the human body?

Books to Read

▲ Read about the cells in the human body.

▲ Read about the human body and how it works.

▲ Read amazing facts about your body.

Glossary

KEY CONCEPT

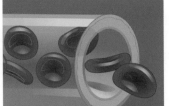

blood vessel (page 22)
A tube that carries blood through the body
A blood vessel carries three kinds of cells.

carbon dioxide (page 13)
A gas that is given off by cells
She releases carbon dioxide when she breathes out.

KEY CONCEPT

cell (page 4)
The smallest living part of a plant or animal
A cell is the smallest living part of your body.

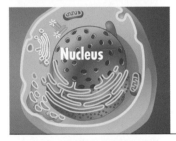

Nucleus

nucleus (page 8)
The part of a cell that tells the cell what to do
The nucleus controls what happens in a cell.

nutrient (page 12)
A substance in food that your body needs to live and grow
You get nutrients from food.

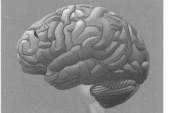

organ (page 11)
A group of tissues that does a job in the body
The brain is an organ.

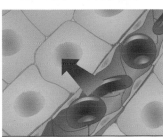

organelle (page 8)
A part of a cell that does a certain job within the cell
One kind of organelle gives cells energy.

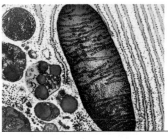

oxygen (page 13)
A gas needed by cells
Blood cells carry oxygen through your body.

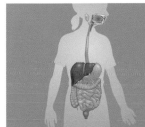

system (page 12)
A group of organs that work together
The digestive system breaks down food.

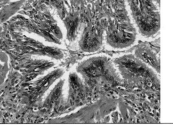

tissue (page 10)
A group of cells that work together
Lung tissue is made of lung cells.

Index